The Harvest of  a Quiet Eye

Patience Strong

The Harvest of
a Quiet Eye

Photographs by Ronald Goodearl
Drawings by Barry Gurbutt

"In common things that round us lie
Some random truths he can impart,
The harvest of a quiet eye
That sleeps and broods on his own heart"

Wm. Wordsworth

FREDERICK MULLER LIMITED
LONDON

First published in Great Britain in 1969 by
Frederick Muller Limited, London, NW2 6LE

Copyright © 1969 Patience Strong

Reprinted 1974, 1979

ISBN 0 584 10760 9

Printed in Great Britain by
Biddles Ltd., Guildford, Surrey

Contents

Dear Guardian Angel

DEAR Guardian Angel, walk with me. My guard and my companion be . . . Prevent, preserve and intervene—where there are dangers unforeseen.

Dear Guardian Angel, close remain—my wayward spirit to restrain—when blindly I go blundering—away from your protective wing.

Dear Angel . . . When I'm called to take—the journey that we all must make. Your final blessing be bestowed—and guide me down the homeward road.

Changing Course

WHEN you're hurt by something done or said—Try to think of something nice instead—to divert the stream of bitterness—from the rocks of anger or excess.

Try to recollect affection shown—the loving gesture and the gentle tone. Often you avoid catastrophe—by changing course and steering quietly—into calmer waters of the mind—forgetting words ungrateful and unkind.

When God sends
a Beautiful Day

SOMEHOW the world seems a wonderful place. There's an excitement that quickens the pace . . . Suddenly everyone's smiling and gay—When God sends a beautiful day.

You cannot explain it, you do not know why —but things look quite different when from the sky—the sun in its glory from Heaven looks down—pouring its blessings on country and town.

The troubles that yesterday weighed on your mind—seem unimportant. You leave them behind . . . The future looks bright and your cares melt away—when God sends a beautiful day.

The Carnival

THE nation may be burdened by a load of dreary care—but Nature takes no notice of disaster or despair—She continues unconcerned her carnival of bloom. What is it to her—this talk of deficit and doom?

Nature's mood is happy, reckless, generous and gay. The air is filled with birdsong from the dawn till close of day . . . Nature decks the trees with blossom, crimson, pink and white— scattering her riches in a frenzy of delight.

God is in His Heaven sing the birds from leafy towers. Everything is young again proclaim the bursting flowers . . . Man alone is sunk in gloom with no good news to tell— while God's other creatures are declaring—All is well.

River Thames at Bourne End, Buckinghamshire

Not All Plain Sailing

LIFE cannot be all plain sailing—that calls for no effort from you. Just drifting in summery weather with never a cloud in the blue.

You never can tell in the morning what sort of day it will be. Although it begins in calm waters, a storm may blow up suddenly, to land you in all kinds of trouble. So know how to handle your sails—gliding along in the sunshine or steering a course through the gales. Ready for changing direction, unruffled when put to the test, by failure, success or misfortune. Prepared for the worst and the best.

When you get to the End of a Dream

WHEN you get to the end of a dream—and the future looks hopeless and grey—Things are never as bad as they seem—though your heart may be breaking today.

You will soon see the sun shining through—though at first it is only a gleam. . . . Never say life is over for you—when you come to the end of a dream.

All Our Days are Numbered

ALL our days are numbered but it's not for us to know—just how many days are left. So don't let this one go—unmarked by something good or lovely, something true or fine—something that redeems it with a touch of the divine.

Think a thought that lifts your mind on to a higher track. Do the thing that takes a load from someone else's back . . . Say the word that changes conflict into harmony. Strike the note that turns the discord into melody.

Take this day out of its groove. Before you let it go—Give to it a meaning and a glory. Let it glow! There are many little ways in which it's possible—to sanctify the commonplace and make it beautiful.

West Meon, Hampshire

The Rose

I SAW a rose in the morning mist through a haze of pearly light. I saw it again when its flame-red heart had opened, warm and bright . . . I noted its beauty—remembering the corner where it grew—and when you came in the starry dusk I picked that rose for you.

'Twas only a tiny episode in the chapter of the day—but as I stood at the cottage gate and watched you walk away—It seemed that there was a hidden meaning charged with destiny. So late you came. So late—Too late to share the best with me.

Too late for Love and for its flowering in the blaze of noon—the raptures and the agonies of life's flamboyant June . . . But is this not the best—this quiet bliss, untouched by tears; this afterglow of friendship in the sunset of the years?

*The Churchyard,
Cookham, Berkshire*

Follow Me

NEVER heed the sceptics or the cynics who deny—truths that have withstood the storms of ages rolling by . . . They who doubt the Word of God have nothing to replace—the wisdom, the philosophy, the glory and the grace—of the Truth proclaimed to man in little Galilee—Valid for the passing needs of every century.

Times may change as change they must, but Truth can never be—subject to the fads and fashions of humanity . . . Truth eternal shines above the turmoil and the strife—in the form of One who was Himself the Way, the Life.

None before or since has said the things He came to say. He spoke for future generations and for this, our day . . . when He taught upon the hills and preached beside the sea—the simple gospel of the Kingdom, saying "Follow me".

You go on Pretending

YOU go on pretending it's not really there—
that tingly Octobery tang in the air. That
smell of a bonfire that comes on the breeze—
the flame and the gold on the shrubs and the
trees. . . . You try not to notice the rose-petals
strewn—over the grave of the glories of June—
refusing to mark how the creeper has thinned—
under the comb of the blustery wind.

You go on deceiving your own foolish heart
—though dahlias blacken and wither apart—
touched by the frost at the morning's sharp
edge—you try not to notice those gaps in the
hedge. . . . You hug your illusions though days
are still bright—but you know—yes you know
that the calendar's right. The Summer you
longed for has come to an end—and now it is
Autumn. What use to pretend?

But never one like this

THERE'LL be other days, my dear, but never one like this. Never shall we know again this mood, the special bliss—of seeing golden leaves against a blue October sky—watching how they quiver as the wind goes dancing by.

You and I together walking in an autumn wood. Could there ever be a day so wonderful, so good? A day to hold and to remember to the very last. A day to treasure in the heart when other dreams have passed.

There'll be better things to do and lovelier things to see—but the present moment will remain the best for me—because it has a magic that defies analysis. There'll be other days, my dear, but never one like this.

A Blessing
and a Promise

SOFTLY, imperceptibly the snowflakes fall and spread—a warm and lovely blanket on the living and the dead. The kindly years like snowflakes fall and cover quietly—the bitterness that lies within the grave of memory.

Winter does not last for ever nor does grief remain—when Time has done its healing work and Spring has come again . . . Love lives on and Life comes back the spirit to renew—wherever there's an open door to let the glory through.

Nigh two thousand years ago the Saviour came to bring—a promise and a blessing to the sad and sorrowing . . . He alone can calm the heart and lift the sunken head. "Blessed are they who mourn," said He, "for they shall be comforted."

Wisdom Without Words

A GARDEN is a Bible where the seeing eye can read—the hidden parables of God in soil and sap and seed . . . The caterpillar and the worm, the blossom and the bee—reveal the deep and sacred secrets of Divinity.

A garden is an open page where those who seek may learn—something from the regal lily and the humble fern . . . The grass, the ant, the butterflies, the pollen and the birds—teach us lessons without books and wisdom without words.

Midsummer Madness

IT'S midsummer madness to think you can hold the song and the sunshine, the blue and the gold, the year at its brightest, the year at its noon, the days that are crowned with the glory of June.

It's midsummer madness to think that the years can pass without heartache and trouble and tears. Your life you can't halt at the point of its prime; you have to give way to the logic of Time. Expect it; accept it. And go bravely on, not looking back at the joys that have gone: the love and the laughter, the wine and the cream. You have to press onward and dream a new dream, to take a new road and to sing a new tune, saying goodbye to the roses of June.

Let Everything Stop

JUST for a moment let everything stop. For a few seconds let everything drop. Sit you right down for a minute or two—and hear what the good Lord is saying to you.

Time's spared for things less important and so—make time for this and let everything go . . . No one's too busy to snatch here and there—a moment for quiet, a moment for prayer . . . Close down on worries and shut up the shop. Your mind needs a breather. Let everything stop!

The Household Cavalry at Windsor

Our Britain

BRITAIN is the loveliest, the loveliest of all.
Here the world is mirrored in an island
green and small—for here God made in minia-
ture the beauties seen elsewhere—Lakeland,
Devon, Skye and Severn: scenes beyond
compare.

Mountain, river, wold and woodland,
beaches, cliffs and downs. The village green, the
winding lane, the little country towns. . . . This
the land that we have fought to save and worked
to keep. It is ours, so let us guard it lest our
children weep—over what has been destroyed
in this destructive age. Cherish it in trust for
them. It is their heritage.

Lovely Day

O LOVELY day when everything—con-spires to make a sad heart sing. O lovely day of sun-bright skies—of fiery flowers with golden eyes—and fruit aflush upon the spray. O lovely day! O lovely day!

A day that promises so much. Awake me with a magic touch and bring me back to life again. After drought, the healing rain.

I see the rose beside the door—as something never seen before. The blackbird singing in the tree—is singing, so it seems, for me . . . The long dark night has passed away. O lovely day! O lovely day!

That's why God made Flowers

FLOWERS can speak the language of the heart. Flowers a quiet message can impart ... Love's most secret thoughts they can convey —telling what no lips can ever say.

Flowers can heal a hurt and flowers can bless —giving comfort, hope and happiness ... Flowers perform a silent ministry—bringing peace, affection, sympathy.

There are things that cannot be confessed. Things that go too deep to be expressed—by tongue or pen in life's most poignant hours— of joy or sorrow. That's why God made flowers.

Revival

A^T Whitsuntide we celebrate the birthday of
the Church. In vain men strive to find a
creed, in book and brain they search—for the
life that satisfies, the truth that makes men free
—A kingdom that was promised based on love
and harmony.

The Church was born at Pentecost on that
first Whitsuntide—when the Spirit came to
bless, to comfort and to guide—rushing like a
mighty wind upon the crowd below—speaking
with a tongue of fire that set their hearts aglow.

Come, O Holy Spirit, come. Revive us with
thy breath. We are emptied of desire, our
souls are cold as death . . . Warm us. Give us
life to rise repentant and restored—to proclaim
a living faith in the arisen Lord.

The Fragrance of Goodwill

IT'S the warming of the sun that draws the fragrance up—from new-mown grass and freshly furrowed clay . . . it's the warmth that lures the scent out of the flowery cup—that opens to the glory of the day.

It's the warmth of loving thoughts that melts the icicle—in hearts where grief has left a bitter chill . . . it's the warming touch of love that works the miracle—and conjures forth the fragrance of goodwill.

He will Send the Rain

LIFT the cup of your empty heart for God to fill again—Hold it up in a time of drought and He will send the rain . . . Catch the blessings as they fall. Their coming may be slow——but day by day the cup will fill and life will overflow—with a quiet happiness you never knew before. Raise the dry cup by an act of faith for Him to fill once more.

He knows how you bore your burden through a desert of despair—finding no green oasis and no well of comfort there . . . He knows how you went on bravely overladen and hard-pressed. He knows how you finished the last long mile—and now He bids you rest—Turn from the struggle and the strain. Let strife and striving cease—enjoying the evening of the years—contented and at peace.

The Secret Garden

SPEAK if you must while I show you round
the garden that I love—wandering by the
heather banks where the branches arch above
. . . Speak of the weather or whatsoever comes
into your mind—as we stroll together where the
mossy pathways wind.

But when we come to the corner where the
guardian trees enclose—the secret place where
it's always spring and no wind of winter blows
—Speak no word by the quiet pool where the
sifted sunlight gleams—and softly tread on the
time-worn stones . . . for you walk amongst
my dreams.

Marriage is Making a Dream Come True

MARRIAGE is sharing with smiles and tears—whatever may come with the changing years . . . Marriage is learning what life can be—when two hearts beat in harmony.

Marriage is building from day to day—a home that's a place where you both can stay—happy together, contented there—whether the weather be foul or fair.

Marriage is loving unfailingly. Marriage is kindness and loyalty . . . Marriage is making a dream come true—and keeping the dream forever new.

The Quiet Room

I̲T'S good to have a quiet room, a room that's bright and warm—where you rest in safety at the centre of a storm. When the wind blows ragged cloud across a leaden sky—and the window rattles as the gale goes howling by . . . And so it is in Life. When hurt by something done or said—and a sudden storm of anger thunders overhead—it is good if in the whirling turmoil of the mind—you can shut out everything that's cruel and unkind—and make a peace within yourself where you can be content—to wait until the worst is over and the storm is spent.

The Faithful Few

ABOVE the fears and tears and troubles of humanity, the Easter Cross is lifted up for every man to see. This, the symbol of the Love that came to meet our need. This, the message and the meaning of the Christian creed.

Nail and hammer could not kill the Love that burned within—the heart of Him in whom there was no hatred and no sin. When upon the Roman cross the wounded Hands were laid—the price demanded of that Love was well and truly paid.

Through the noonday darkness as the tortured Saviour died—the faithful few remained to keep their vigil at His side. And so today; the faithful few stand by to watch and pray—waiting for the risen Christ; the Lord of Easter Day.

You Can't

YOU can't put a star in your pocket. You can't hoard your dreams on a shelf . . . You can't net a sunbeam in passing and catch it to keep for yourself.

You can't collect dewdrops like diamonds. One touch and they vanish away . . . You can't hold your happiest moments like butterflies pinned for display.

You can't lock a thought in a cupboard—or pinion a hope by its wings . . . You can't keep in banks or in boxes—life's greatest and loveliest things.

Lenten Bells

THE snowdrops ring their tiny bells when Lenten weather brings the sound of morning birdsong and the fluttering of wings. With stalks of tender green and petals white as virgin snows—their fragile beauty lends a magic to the winter's close.

Overnight they seem to burst out of the sodden clay. Small and frail and fairylike they brave the coldest day: a miracle of resurrection, life defying death. Sweet the music of their chimes upon the wind's wild breath.

Little bells of Lent—beneath the leafless trees they ring a carillon of joy that bids my heart awake and sing . . . March goes storming by with icy blast and skies of grey but once the snowdrops have appeared, can spring be far away?

Summer Butterfly

HAPPINESS is something like a summer butterfly—First it's here and then it's there, forever flitting by—never settling anywhere, but always on the wing. It can't be bought or caught or pinioned: an elusive thing.

So when God sends happiness don't question how or why. Take it where you find it. Thankful be, and never try—to understand from whence it comes. Enjoy the present hour. Happiness is rare and is as fleeting as a flower.

Seek it and you miss it, but it seems to come your way—when you least expect it. You awake one lovely day—to find a new song in your heart, a new light in the sky. Seize the golden moment. It is only passing by.

Little Things

CHILDREN, puppies, lambs, calves, chicks and all defenceless things—need the touch of gentle hands and warm protective wings . . . Helpless they are born into a world of cruelty—where it seems there's little time for loving sympathy.

Let us never lack compassion for the small and weak. They are at our mercy. For themselves they cannot speak . . . Feed them, guard them, meet their needs and ease their sufferings. God relies on us to care for all His little things.

Out into the Light

I TOOK a path through a tangled wood where the trees hung thick and low—making a web of shadow shutting out the sun's warm glow—but I followed the thread of that little path till at last it led me through—to a sunlit place where the trees stood back to reveal a lovely view.

I took a path through the wood of life when my heart was sad and sore—knowing not where it led for I had never come before—along that path to walk alone in sorrow night and day—moving through the darkness on a strange and lonely way . . . but suddenly came an angel touch to comfort and to bless—that guided me to a quiet place of peace and happiness . . . If we cast our care on Him and walk by faith, not sight—God will always bring us through and out into the light.

And Yet—I Love Thee, Lord

FORGIVE me, Lord, when day by day I offer unto Thee—things unworthy of the Love that thou hast given me; poor and fragmentary worship, gifts of no great price—things that cost me nothing in the way of sacrifice.

Forgive me, Lord, for bringing Thee the remnant of my powers—tired and wearied by my pleasures in the day's last hours—instead of rising in the freshness of the morning air to offer Thee the first fruits of a heart aglow with prayer.

Lord, I give so little. I am sparing with my praise. In Thy service I should spend the best of all my days—and yet I grudge the measured time. Much more I could afford. I am mean and miserly . . . and yet—I love Thee, Lord.

Half the Trouble

HALF the trouble in this age of crime and vice and strife—comes because so many seldom touch the springs of life: children pent in flats who never knew the ecstasy—of paddling in a running brook or scrambling up a tree . . . They never see a foal, a pig, a cow, a field of wheat. Their stunted minds are starved, their education incomplete—because they never see the gold of buttercups in May—or hear a lark make angel music on a lovely day. Pity them—who never walk the woods or climb the downs. The lost, the disinherited: the children of the towns.

Under the Law

THERE are basic laws at work within the cosmic frame. The tides, the stars, the seasons. Light and darkness, ice and flame . . . God so made the Universe. No order could there be if chance and chaos reigned instead of law and harmony . . . Man is also under law, the moral law that brings—pain and retribution in the wake of evil things.

River Avon at
Christchurch, Hampshire

Fishing

WHAT did I catch with my rod and line?
Nothing. Of fish there was never a sign—
but more than content I made my way—with
empty basket home that day.

I caught something better: I caught the sigh
—of reeds that swayed as the wind went by.
I caught not fish, but the breath of flowers—
and the song of larks in the sky's blue bowers
. . . The country magic, the gold, the green.
The healing peace of that quiet scene . . . and a
wonderful memory there I caught—on the line
of a long and lovely thought.

Lost

LOST between daybreak and sundown—the hour that I idled away. Gold from Time's treasury squandered. One precious hour of the day.

Sixty good minutes I wasted. Where did they go? Where indeed? Minutes I'll never recover—minutes that someday I'll need.

Life does not tick on forever—as all have to learn to their cost . . . We cannot recapture a moment—or call back the time that we lost.

NE QUID PEREAT

VIII
VII
VI
V

I   II   III   IIII

HORAS NON NUMERO NISI SERENAS

Sundial at Marlow Buckinghamshire

Let Well Alone

LET well alone. It is wiser the pathway of peace to pursue. Gloss over the failings of others and hope they do likewise for you. Never rake over old quarrels. Let sleeping dogs lie where they lie. If something should vex or annoy you, endeavour to turn a blind eye.

Never go looking for trouble, for sooner or later no doubt—you'll find it without ever searching, for trouble is always about. Do not provoke touchy people and say what you know will offend. He who hangs on to a grievance soon finds that he hasn't a friend.

You're bound to get hurt in the scramble of life with its jolts and its jars, but don't make too much of your bruises and don't go round counting your scars. Where there's been strife and contention, don't dig up the long-buried bone. If everything's going on smoothly—be thankful and let well alone.

The Fountain

IN the long-neglected garden stood the fountain dry and bare. No lovely jet of sparkling water rose into the summer air, to splash into the lily pools where dragonflies lay quivering. Without the water the fountain died; a lump of stone, a cold dead thing.

In a long-neglected house a life was lived walled in by grief. A grudge was harboured in the heart, a grievance nursed without relief. The springs of happiness were choked and love denied in all its ways. How sad when a soul dries up and dies like a fountain where no water plays!

The Promise

THIS is what the blackbird promised me—
one bitter day when all seemed cold and
dead. He prophesied that one day there would
be—a canopy of blossom overhead—and
underfoot a carpet deep and bright—of primroses and violets thickly spread. Where once
snow lay encrusted sugar-white—There'd be
bluebells . . . This is what he said.

I stood beside the frosted windowpane—and
listened to the thing he had to say. His golden
notes came slipping through the rain. The wind
was rough, the sky was dark and grey—and
from his perch in branches bare and black—He
said—Though winter lingers grim and long—
One blue April morning I'll come back—and
sing to you a sweeter lovelier song.

The Magic of the Sea

THERE'S something in the magic of the sea—
that stirs the heart, evoking history. You
call to mind the men who sailed afar—beyond
the safety of the harbour bar—to make new
Englands under alien skies.

Men of faith and valiant enterprise ... And
they who when the call of freedom came—
sailed out to save us from defeat and shame ...
These things come back on tides of memory.
There's something in the magic of the sea.

Near Lymington,
Hampshire

That Old-Fashioned Thing

I KNEW it was meant, this strange meeting of ours. I knew it was meant from the start. I knew it was something that fate had ordained. I knew it deep down in my heart.

I knew that our stars had been leading to this. I knew it the moment we met. In wonderful ways that I could not explain, I knew that my course had been set.

What is the magic that brought you along— to that place at that time and by chance? I can't understand, so we'll say it was this: that old-fashioned thing called romance.

Life's Unfinished Symphony

LIFE is like an uncompleted symphony that goes—on and on eternally. The music ebbs and flows . . . sometimes sweet and lovely, sometimes sad and full of tears—changing with the changing rhythms of the passing years.

You think that all is over when a little thing goes wrong. You think that it has ended with the ending of the song. You say your heart has broken when bereaved you sit alone. The melody of life is drowned by sorrow's undertone.

There is silence for a time, a pause for memory—then the music starts again, but in a different key . . . You think God has forsaken you, that everything has gone—but another theme begins. The symphony goes on.

Heritage

LEAVE us a few little copses. Do not sweep them all away—where the primroses bloom in April and the bluebells come out in May. Leave us the woods and the meadows where the children can climb and play and get to know God's small creatures, learning the natural way.

Leave us a few little corners, where the leafy pathways wind, for we need what the trees can give us: health and healing and peace of mind. Leave us our unspoilt village—with its church and cricket green—for history lies in the beauty of this quiet English scene.

Wherever the good land is threatened, resist, protest, complain. Build round the towns if it's needed, but leave us the country lane. The pastures, the fields and the orchards. The earth that supplies what we need. The country is ours for our keeping: a heritage precious indeed.

Water End,
Hertfordshire

A Heart Without a Hurt

A HEART without a hurt in it is like an empty well. A heart that never knew a grief is like a hollow shell—where nothing ever wakes an echo to revive again—the long forgotten memory of ecstasy or pain.

The eyes that never shed a tear of pity or regret—are the eyes of someone who has never really met—face to face with Life and with the challenge that it brings—seen through other people's troubles, tears and sufferings.

The one who never had a scar can never understand—the compulsion of compassion and of Love's demand . . . He has missed the inner meaning at the core of things. A heart that never suffers is a heart that never sings.

The Reconciling Word

EVERY time an evil force is challenged and subdued—The Lord is resurrected and His power on earth renewed. Every time Love triumphs over sin and selfishness—He comes forth out of the dark to brighten and to bless.

Every time a loving thought, as soft as angel wings—brings its quiet strength to bear upon Satanic things—Goodness triumphs. Life is lifted to a higher plane. The drama of redemption is enacted once again.

There is joy in Heaven when the word of Love is said: With the reconciling word Christ rises from the dead—and walks amongst us once again revealed, revived, restored—Clothed in Easter glory, risen King and living Lord.

April Rain

UNDER the kiss of the April rain—the old earth comes alive again—young and fresh and beautiful—decked as for a carnival . . . The blossoms thicken on the spray. The hedges quicken by the way. A primrose tapestry is spread—on laneside bank and garden bed.

The earth's old face that bore the sign—of winter's frown is now ashine—with smiles that radiate a glow—where daffodils and lilacs blow —and wallflowers by the path unfold—yellow, amber, red and gold.

In the dawn the bird choirs raise—anthems of ecstatic praise. In the heart joy leaps anew. The dream of spring has all come true—for under the kiss of the April rain—the tired old earth is young again.

The Little Shop

EVERYBODY loves the little shop where you can buy—onions, stockings, cheese and stamps, a loaf, a comb, a pie: a shop run by a family, a cosy sort of place, where you find a word of welcome and a smiling face.

Here one hears enquiries over Mrs. Jones's toe. How's old Mr. Smith today and when's the Flower Show? Don't forget tomorrow's meeting at the Rectory. The human harmless gossip of a small community . . . At the counter friends and neighbours greet throughout the year. The little shops of England! May they never disappear.

Moreton-in-Marsh, Gloucestershire

Nine Times out of Ten

NINE times out of ten life seems to work out for the best. Nine times out of ten you find that if you let things rest—Providence will sort them out without your helping hand—Not perhaps exactly in the way that you had planned —but in a wiser way and from a broader point of view. So do not try to force events or push your own plans through . . . Cease to worry. Trust and pray. Though things look black as night—Nine times out of ten you find that everything comes right.

They Too Loved Life

THEY too loved life, the hearth, the home.
They too knew what it was to roam—by
dappled wood and dimpled stream. They too
knew what it was to dream.

They too loved life and felt desire—upspring-
ing from the heart's warm fire . . . They too
once knew the taste of bliss—a child's delight,
a woman's kiss . . . And yet they turned aside
to die—in sand and sea and flaming sky . . .
That we might live.

Waddesdon, near Aylesbury, Buckinghamshire

At Maidenhead
Berkshire

Tell Me

TELL me how a seagull glides with such an easy grace. Tell me, how do migrants through the trackless heavens trace—a path above the seas and mountains with their tiny wings? Tell me how a nest is built and why a skylark sings.

Tell me how a blossom bursts out of a leafless tree. Tell me how the earth revolves, for it's a mystery . . . Tell me what puts life into the beating heart of man—and how the power of love can change it. Tell me if you can.

A Quiet Moment Here and There

IF you would advance you must retreat into the calm—to be found within yourself: 'he place where there is balm—for wounded heart and weary spirit. Only there you find—easement for the strains and stresses of the daily grind.

If you would go forward you must take a few steps back—deep into the inner world to seek the thing you lack. There in silence absolute to hold and to possess—the precious pearl of quietude, the jewel of happiness.

Don't go rushing on non-stop. You need a break each day—to relieve the tension, to reflect, to rest, to pray. . . . Minds and bodies cannot stand the worry and the wear—of modern life without a quiet moment here and there.

Unwritten Music

THE loveliest of music, the sweetest songs of all are the songs that no man ever wrote: the wild ecstatic singing of a waterfall—thrush's vesper, blackbird's morning note.

The sigh of wind in wheatfields, the ripplings of the streams—the changing tones of calm or angry seas . . . the hum of bees in summer and the secret themes—played upon the harpstrings of the trees.

Everywhere you hear it if you are listening. For you the hidden orchestra will play—the unwritten music and every bird will sing— above the raucous babel of the day.

Conquest

DEEP and far and wide man casts his net—
but himself he has not mastered yet—He
walks in space and treads the starry skies—
but lacks the wit and wisdom to devise—a way
of life to live successfully—in a world of peace
and harmony.

For all his clever tricks he cannot boast—a
triumph in the things that matter most. He has
not won the battle of the mind—or he would
be wise and good and kind ... To conquer
mighty Nature is his goal—and yet his little
self he can't control.

Overburdened

MINUTE by minute throughout the night
the snowflakes fall and weigh—gently
and yet heavily on branch and twig and spray—
and sometimes when the icy burden can't be
shaken free—a laden bough will bend and
break and spoil a lovely tree.

Minute by minute throughout our lives the
world and its affairs—presses upon us with a
weight of little fears and cares—that often
prove too much for us unless we learn to pray—
for wisdom sufficient to bear with joy the bur-
dens of the day.

Life still has a Meaning

IF there is a future there is time for mending—
time to see your troubles coming to an ending . . . Life is never hopeless however great
your sorrow—if you're looking forward to a
new tomorrow.

If there's time for wishing then there's time
for hoping—when through doubt and darkness
you are blindly groping . . . Though the heart
be heavy and hurt you may be feeling—if there's
time for praying there is time for healing.

So if through your window there's a new day
breaking—thank God for the promise, though
mind and soul be aching—If with harvest over
there's grain enough for gleaning—there is a
tomorrow and life still has a meaning.

Look at Me

"LOOK at me," says the tulip, "if you are feeling low—discouraged or disgruntled, and life has lost its glow . . . Be like me," says the tulip, "lift up your empty cup—waiting for the sunshine to come and fill it up.

"Look at me," says the tulip. "Stand calm and straight and strong—unruffled and unbroken when rough winds blow along . . . You, too, are God's creation. You, too, are wonderful. A human, like a flower, is a living miracle.

"I live to make life lovely for all who come my way. I do not strive or struggle, but quietly day by day—I grow within the compass of the plan ordained for me: to adorn the corner where I was meant to be."

The Poor

THE poor are those who never ever hear a nightingale—or the murmur of a streamlet in a lonely dale—the bleat of lambs, the drowsy humming of the honey bees—the sigh of wind in swaying corn, the roar of stormy seas.

The poor are those who never see a wild rose in a hedge—or the quivering of rushes at a river's edge . . . The poor are those who never smell the earth in summer rain—or the scent of honeysuckle at a windowpane.

The really poor aren't those who never have a coin to spare—They are those who never walk on grass or breathe fresh air . . . who divorced from Nature's laws lack life's intrinsic wealth—the simple joy that is the source of happiness and health.

Go the Quiet Way

YOU have to seek the quiet ways if Nature you would know. You have to find the secret paths, the little tracks that go—into unfrequented places far from fumes and crowds—the lonely valleys and the hills that hide amongst the clouds.

If you want to taste the peace that God alone can give—you have to seek before you find. You have to learn to live—calm amidst the trouble and the turmoil of the day—Through chaos and confusion you must go the quiet way.

The Afterglow

LOVELIEST of memories! Stay on inside my heart—whatever else may fade away as passing years depart—Linger like the fragrance of a rose at summer's height—never failing to evoke perpetual delight.

Loveliest of memories! that glorious golden day—that perfect day of happiness with sunshine all the way—when everything was wonderful—when life and love were new—and just like a fairytale a lovely dream came true.

Time may dim the colours. Things must change as days go on—but when the glow has faded and the first gay rapture gone—The afterglow of happiness together we'll recall: the loveliest of memories: the loveliest of all.